The Map That Lies Between Us

New and Collected Poems
1980–2000

Anne Carroll George

Black Belt Press
Montgomery

Black Belt Press
P.O. Box 551
Montgomery, AL 36101

Library of Congress Cataloging-in-Publication Data:
George, Anne.
The map that lies between us : new and collected poems,
1980-2000 / Anne Carroll George.
p. cm.
ISBN 1-880216-88-4
I. Title.
PS3557.E469 M37 2000
811'.54—dc21
00-009748

Design by Jennifer Marcato
Printed in the United States of America

01 03 04 02 00
2 4 5 3 1

The Black Belt, defined by its dark, rich soil, stretches across central Alabama. It was the heart of the cotton belt. It was, and is, a place of great beauty, of extreme wealth and grinding poverty, of pain and joy. Here we take our stand, listening to the past, looking to the future.

For Dilly

Contents

The Edge of the World

Some of It Is True

Spraying Under the Bed for Wolves

Wild Goose Chase

Acknowledgments

Grateful acknowledgment is given to the following journals and magazines in which some of these poems first appeared: *Negative Capability*, *Elk River Review*, *South Coast Poetry Journal*, *Kalliope*, *Aura*, *Light*, *Snake Nation Review*, *Alabama Arts*, *Dear Magnolia*, *Alalitcom*, *Mobile Bay Monthly*, *A Baker's Dozen*, and *Ordinary and Sacred As Blood: Alabama women speak*.

"The Grist Mill," "Playing Bingo at the Elks' Club," and "The Old Woman As Rose, Mountain, Wind" each received a Hackney Award. "My Mother Candling Eggs" was nominated for the Pushcart Prize, 1992, by *Kalliope*.

Special thanks to the Alabama State Council on the Arts for an individual artist's fellowship grant that aided in the completion of this work.

Some of It Is True
Curbow Publications, 1993

Spraying Under the Bed for Wolves
Druid Press, 1985

Wild Goose Chase
Druid Press, 1982

The Edge of the World

Late, Daniel's Bend

Twilight oils the water, slicks
the riverbank's rose veins. I
sit on the pier, waiting, watching
while white tips of waves fade
and one blue heron, dark on dark,
still stalks the shallow reeds.

And then downstream the sound of oars,
muffled laughter, one lantern shining.
And I rise to meet you, to take your net,
my body fragile as a pale blue knife
in a world hurtling through stars.

This, then, is the moment of turning,
with everything coming in home before dark.
This, then, is what sustains us, this
blessed burden of being human,
as you take my hand and we go in
and night closes its great door.

❧

Picture of My Parents

The month before they separate, they sit
on my grandparents' steps, his arm
around her shoulder, her hand on his leg.
The summer sun of 1931 reflects
on their dark hair, his parted in the middle,
slicked down, hers bobbed. They do not smile
for the camera. Instead their young faces
seem caught by surprise—almost frightened.

In the shadow of the porch behind them
I stand, slightly out of focus.
Three years old, almost, I watch them,
my hand held up in a goodbye wave as if,
knowing their story's ending, I
am leaving the picture, leaving
to grow old as they will not,
waving quietly so I won't startle them.

❧

For a Sister 13 Years Younger

Let us say you weren't, as Aunt Mona
whispered, taken from Mother blue,
waxy as the cord around your throat,
but yelling, red, swollen with life.
Let us say, there was never a small casket,
that you called me tonight, Sister, while I
was cooking supper and I walked around
the kitchen, telephone to ear, listening
to your day, your familiar accent,
our mother's accent, little blue wax doll,
little child whose grave I,
still the only child, cried over,
looking around to see who watched.
I could invite you over to eat,
give you another cutting of Mother's
Christmas Cactus and find out when
or if you are ever going to marry
that man you've been with so long.
"Sister," I would say, "Sister,"
willing you to step into the name,
to become what you never were
in this space that widens beside me.

Lettie's Song

for my grandmother

Light lingers, green to gold to first cold
star light star bright. And Lettie
steps from the pocked bones of the poplars,
hands cupped round her rounded belly,
the cradle where her child quickens.
Her pale hair is caught with ribbons
that flare and fade in the late breeze
while she hums a song to the unborn,
of smoke-dry sun, starfish, towers,
light that burrows through stone.
Sing, Lettie, sing to your child,
the blue moth that takes your breath.
Sing how living surprises us all
as you hold your palm to the innocent moon,
your life, your death.

Late Fruit

for Emelda

At Rehab in over-sixty aqua aerobics
we do the rainbow stretch and crab walk and
lean on the bar for the flutter kick. Sunshine
falls through the skylight and dissolves
in warm water, sweet to old scars.
My sisters, we are stories rich for telling:
the giant teddy bear man who came late
to your life and believed you beautiful,
the grandchild you thought you would never have,
your heart held gently in a stranger's palm.
Look at the girl eating an apple
and watching us through the gym window.
She sees our gray hair and bent bodies
and probably thinks that given a choice
we would turn time around,
live our lives backwards. Some day
she will learn what we already know,
    we women, we survivors,
late autumn fruit is surprisingly sweet.

Poetry Shards

I have a closet full of them
saving them for some giant mosaic
where all the pieces will fit
just so
and one day I'll do it,
glue them together, probably
bleed on the sharp ones,
break a few of the fragile ones,
and God knows what I'll end up with
but it will be something,
some thing
I will breathe on and polish
until it sparks and comes alive.
Then I will know its name.

My Grandmother's Story

Try living with someone sixty years, child,
there'll be more missing than a finger.
That's no lie.
And him saying, "Oh, Alice, I'm bleeding to death,"
staggering around like a stuck pig.
And me saying, "You are not,"
which of course he wasn't,
and going to fetch the coal oil.
But, you know, that man still blames me,
says I ruined his handwriting, of all things.
A plain lie.
Three-fourths of the blood was from that chicken
which nobody even noticed was still flopping around
and which the old fool should have held tighter.

I'll tell you this, though, about his finger.
When he quit pointing, things got better.

For Gerry, the Other Angel

Imagine us as angels, coat-hanger wings
and tinsel halos, standing guard
over baby Jesus in the heat and odd shadows
of the candlelit church. My uncle
took our picture. Remember? He laughed
and said this was one for the books
just before we marched down the aisle
daring each other to order the shepherds
to run like hell to Bethlehem,
chickening out, of course. "Behold!"
we said to our smiling families,
"We bring tidings of great joy."
And as one, they whispered, "Angels.
These children are angels!" But we were ten
and thought it wonderful when a Wise Man
keeled over, toppling both crib and kneeling Mary.

If I told you I found the picture
all these decades later of two angels,
one dark, one fair, would you believe me?
Would you say, "I hadn't realized."
Gerry, remember how Jesus's head fell off?
How, somehow, that made God possible?

❧

Dancing at the Edge of the World

Let's dance, old man, old love.
Let's dance a slow dance,
a round dance,
here at the edge of the world.
The tide is singing tonight
as it will when no one
remembers us,
and I've forgotten
or forgiven
where I stop and you start.
So let's dance,
holding each other,
moon, sun,
while we dip and circle
to earth's divining hum
and dark, dark water
fixes the stars.

August, Boca Grande

The sun half-high, sea oats, beach plums.
We buy apples and crusty bread
and eat on the shell-strewn beach
where a child in pink shorts flies a kite,
dips and turns, dips and turns.

Held by the thread of the Milky Way,
we lie in warm sand holding hands,
while giant sea turtles slide ashore
to drop their eggs in shallow nests
and the Pleiades showers us with stars.
On the horizon, a fishing boat's light
dips and turns, dips and turns.

The sky opens and morning comes.
The sun has shifted an inch or two.
We take our coffee to the porch,
while gulls, egrets rob tidal pools.
And beyond the sandbar one lone fin
dips and turns, dips and turns.

Virginia Woolf Walks into the Water

I am going mad again, Leonard. The voices
and the river's shining, broken into pieces.
I have left my thick shoes on the riverbank,
black sturdy liars, for I am a word
lost in the middle of a book.
This morning I saw almond blossoms
and quince and wondered how
spring can be sad, heavy
as the rocks in my pockets.
Leonard, no two people have ever been so happy
as we. I see you napping in your chair and
think this is my husband who loves me.
But now I am walking peacefully
toward another form, or nothing—
it matters not which. Leonard,
I can't spoil your life anymore.
The river is cold with an ebb and flow
like the beat of a heart. But my shoes
are dancing. They say, "We stand
on a little island. But, oh,
my dearest, it has been lovely."

Dvorak in Spillville

"I should never have written the symphony like
   I have if I hadn't seen America."
                    —ANTONIN DVORAK, 1893

The old church organ, bought second-hand
carted across the prairie, the light, the sun
slanting through the open door and windows,
afternoon heat, thunderstorms, the Iroquois drums,
the black man singing "Going Home," and
maybe for a moment he thought he was home,
that here in Iowa he had found the center of the world,
Anna without the dream of lost children
and the blood, the butcher's blood of sheep
was washed from his hands
and the world was birds singing
these hands that had been washed with so much
animal's blood and a music to the slaughter,
the knife sharply drawn, the rhythm of sex
and everything was absorbed as everything is
and he is Anna and the summer day and
Josefina, his first love, and his dead children
and his living children and the chords
pour through the windows and over Spillville
so children stop to listen for a moment

and by the river a couple making love
believe the music is the other's body
and women taking clothes from the line
look up into a blue mirror. Hedge rows
bloom with the smell of semen, and Anna,
rising from the afternoon sleep, clutches the air,
lost in the mercy of his music.

Published in *Elk River Review*
1st Place, Red Mountain Rendezvous

POEMS FROM

Some of It Is True

Curbow Publications, 1993

Nightrun

This clear night
our boat
slices the warm Gulf,
our wake
is a white path.
And all the fish that flared
golden in the sun
drift in darkness
while we set our course.

I know our history
is written in light years
and the murmuring tongue
of the Gulf. I know
below us continents shift.
But this clear night
you and I are together
and the stars
how lightly they tether us.

Sagittarius

"Close to the horizon," you say,
pointing southward over the Gulf.
And I say, "Yes," trying to find
the faint constellation. A cold wind
is blowing from the east. We
have left the loud party and
crossed the sand into darkness.
Brittle stars rattle like dice.
Like the ice in my cup. Now,
Above us the centaur aims his bow.

"The fire sign," you say. "You
are a traveler and a philosopher."
And I laugh and take your hand,
calloused and warm, while we walk together
into the night, into whatever is
between the stars, into the arrow's path.

Playing Bingo at the Elks' Club

Try a diamond shape on six cards
after several bourbons to congratulate
the sun which fell into the ocean
in fine form to the applause of the crowd
on the pier. Someone soberer than I
bingos and the crowd sighs, little puffs
of air eddying through smoke that
wanders to the beach to curl
around fishing boats whose captains
are Elks who march between tables
saying "I have a good bingo" and
serving nachos at the concession stand.

A baldheaded man in a canary cardigan
tells me he fought at Okinawa and
all he needs is O-72 which the caller
calls and the man screams bingo
and collects 25 dollars which he waves
in the air saying he will take us all
to Wendy's. But his wife puts the money
in her dhurrie rug bag in the side compartment
with the coupons. Ah, canary man, best not argue
with a woman who carries coupons.

I-19. I cover the square and look outside
where a lopsided moon is caught in the rail

of the Ocaloosa Bridge and the water
is a periwinkle current. Come with me,
canary man. Like you I've known thousands
of October nights. We'll go to the bait shop,
down the dunes. We'll pass the bottle,
talk of Okinawa, of bingo. And when we swim
long young hair will thread itself around us.

The Jetty, December 23

The Gulf churns around and sometimes
over the jumbled rocks. On hands and knees
I climb the slippery surface
to the last flat boulder where I stand
and look around, cold, wet, exhilarated.
Later on I will notice the sky

is the blue of Mama's Depression dishes
and the moon is a white brush stroke.
Angry gulls argue the loss of their roost
and across the inlet a neon sign flashes
BUD AND ALLEY'S, BUD AND ALLEY'S.

But now on the jetty I shout to the sky
that the sun and I have made it another year.
I bless the water and the earth as if,
claiming friendship, I have the right.
And perhaps I do. My outstretched hand
has something to do with tides
and slow burning fires. It has everything
to do with being earthbound, mortal and alive.

Jubilee

The moon spreads like a net over the bay
and the fish rise to the surface
slicing the water's skin
with fins, serrated, glistening.
Their mouths, perfect circles, pop,
wanting oxygen. Water whorls
as they slide against each other
circling, circling into the shallows.

Long after the sun fell into itself
the bay was veined with ochre.
And the people came and scooped up water
threaded with red that smeared
on their hands. They knew to gather
seines and baskets and
put a watchman on the pier.

> *Mimosas open to the moon. Their fragrance*
> *falling through summer windows stirs*
> *sleepers' dreams. Water oaks*
> *move closer to the bay. Mockingbirds*
> *awaken and call out.*

Before the shout of "Jubilee!"
people are running to the water's edge
and the fish see them coming,
feel themselves lifted, water
sliding away like skin.

Their bones lurch against lightness;
their gills fan red with oxygen.
And for a moment only they bloom in balance
in a night they have never known.
"Jubilee! Jubilee!" sing the fishermen
to the millions of moons in the bay.

New Orleans

When we lived in New Orleans
you couldn't sleep and I
would rub your back while the rain,
the impossible rain of New Orleans,
weighted the oleander outside our window
so it brushed tic tic against the pane.
Sometimes we made love matter-of-factly
because we were married and sharing
a mattress. Afterwards, lying apart,
we would hear tugs sounding the river
and the clank of the streetcar down St. Charles.

To this day I think of New Orleans,
how we left when the heaviness
made your bones ache. The hill
is here as you imagined, the scent
of pine resin light in the sun. But I
remember shrimp boiling, diesel fumes,
old flowers. There was something
about New Orleans I almost believed.

❧

Old Men Driving

I love the way old men drive, staring straight ahead,
both hands on the wheel of their Lincolns
or Chryslers. I love the way they steer
close to the center line, stop before intersections,
wait too long at lights. But most of all
I love the wives who sit beside them, purses
clutched in their laps, coupons sorted,
trusting that their husbands, as always,
will get them safely to the grocery.

And when we pull up beside them
I reach for your hand and hold it,
wishing for us such an ending, need,
already knowing how they awaken at night
listening for the other's breathing. And you,
perhaps sharing my thoughts, turn to me,
and we look at each other, startled,
just as the couple next to us must be
at having come so far together.

Davidsohn's Wife

"The SS should be allowed to have a fling."
 —ADOLPH HITLER, Munich, November 9, 1938

Let them call it *kristallnacht.*
The truth will shatter that delicate name
like paving stones hurled through Jews' windows.
"Davidsohn! Davidsohn!" and my world was gone.
Waking to what I thought was dawn and Davi
rushing to the window. "My God! Stay here!"
But I followed, saw the synagogue burning,
saw Davi running, screaming to the firemen
"The sacred objects!" They pushed him away;
he fell just as the curtains of the Ark,
the scrolls, the prayer books were hurled
from the balcony. "Here are your objects,
Rabbi." And I ran to Davi and helped him up
and saw for the first time that he was old,
saw my old hands buttoning his coat,
wiping the blood from his forehead.

And while we stood in that rain of ashes,
While Davi (as he had for thirty years)
recited the Kaddish, I thought I was dreaming,
that I would wake and walk to the window
to see the Rosenthals opening their bakery,
the blue and white awning blinking open
like an eye. And I would press my forehead

against cool perfect glass and
let my nightmares be bleached and bleached
until they were nothing but light.

Miami, 1933

In the late August light
after the sun falls into Biscayne Bay
my father walks down Flagler,
smiles for a street photographer
who mails him the picture two weeks later.
He is thirty years old. The camera
catches him midstep, striding
towards the pier, toward the *El Rio*
that ferries to the Cuban gambling ship.

He is dressed for a party,
dark blazer, white pants.
His hair is parted in the middle,
slicked down. Later, with Olivia,
he will stand by the ferry rail
and point out beaches he will develop.
And Olivia, holding his arm, will see
homes and hotels rising through scrub.
While they drink their beer and
watch lights come on across the channel
he thinks he will marry Olivia
and live with her fifty years.
He has six more Augusts.

But this night as the first stars
drop into the bay and the gambling ship
nears, he doesn't worry about the future,

about deserting a wife and baby
a thousand miles away. Rumba rhythms
lap the ferry and porpoises
silver in the still water.

He writes on the back of his picture
Miami, August, '33. Ten dollars in my pocket.
Olivia sends it to me forty years later,
to the daughter fifteen years older
than the father in the picture.
I look at this man I never knew
who has my son's broad face
and write this poem.

Some of it is true.

For My Friend Who Would Prove Divinity with Numbers

Patient man, you explain so carefully
the significance of numbers in the Bible,
how when the fishermen went out from Galilee
and caught one hundred fifty-three fish
it MEANT something, not just a good day's catch
that any fisherman might envy. You swear
six-six-six and eight-eight-eight abound
so plentifully they should convince unbelievers
like a two by four straight to the head.
And I believe your belief. But I
want mystery, not proof. I want the Grail
glimpsed only by Parsifal. And lying
under the star-ridden sky at night, watching
it turn gently around me, I want no answers
but questions, eternal, human questions
that bear me down until I stretch my hand
to whatever infinity is and say, "My God."

Shark Drive

"Thirty sharks," you say. "Count them."
And I look at the picture, at gray shapes
hanging in the sun-scissored water.
But what I see is you balanced
against the coral cliff, your hand
aiming the camera. And my belly knots.
My son, I bring to this moment years
of parceling out your umbilical cord.

This morning at the jetties you
climbed the rocks and stood in the spray
and I followed, picking my way carefully
up the slippery surface. Three blue herons
soared from the rushes. Eyes shining, you
held out your arms in a blessing.

My child, bless me. You, no longer child,
know the color of my love. Bless your mother
and be wary of me who, in an instant,
would whisk you back inside my body
and waddle down the street, hands pressed
against your stirring, while I smile
and murmur, "Now, now. Now you are safe."

❧

The Grist Mill

Afternoon sun pours over us.
We say only it is a beautiful day
but neither of us would be surprised
if maple leaves drifting to the creek
stayed suspended, small tongues of flame
against blue layered sky.
The mill wheel creaks and turns.
Water leaks from the trough,
pools over smooth sandstone.
The path, too, is smooth,
ochre with iron ore.

A sign almost hidden by chokeberry
and goldenrod says John Wesley Hall
built this mill, 1860, operated it
sixty years. Surely, I think,
there was a day like this for him
with butterflies and blackeyed Susans
when he sat by his dam and watched deer
across the creek and thought he
would never die, that under such a sky
death was impossible. And when wrapping
the day around him like a patchwork quilt
he waded, as we do now, into the stream,
feeling the water, patient, cool
close around his feet.

Crabapple Branches

Sitting on the stile over the dune
I watch the sun touch the horizon.
My radio plays "Stella by Starlight"
and I am thinking of the boy
who made love to me years ago
to this song, how I understood
that he would break my heart
and was already forgiving him, how
later, slipping through the screen door
that whispered "shhh, shhh," I
smelled the crabapple branches
my mother had picked and thought
"I will always remember this."

Now a lifetime later the earth nods
and the last chord of sun
disappears with a green flash.
Soon I will walk home
through thickening air and
the lights will be on and beckoning.

He wrote to me once,
a card from California.
"I am here," was all he said.

Autumn Apples

We hiked to Turkey Creek,
taking a shortcut
through woods that glowed
golden in the sun. On rocks
over the falls, we ate apples,
throwing cores into the water,
laughing as our lips touched.
Then we lay on leaves
that crackled as we
moved together rhythmically.

Now that I sleep
encased in an aging body
strange how you
dominate my dreams —
eighteen—
your tongue tasting of apples.

Fog, Shades Mountain

Past the dogwood, the world ends, gray, swirling,
while in our kitchen the radio plays softly
and you stand at the stove turning eggs.
Somehow it all comes together, the music, the mist,
and I am remembering another morning and
the mountainous road to Mariposa with you
turning toward me touching my hand.
How could I have known then, decades ago,
that I would not love you forever but
in unpredictable stops and starts that
would startle, leave me beguiled as now
watching you cook eggs in our kitchen.

For Earl Who Got a Haircut from a Barber Named Butch with Tattoos

Alice had had a miscarriage (her third)
and wouldn't be in the shop for a while
and her sister said she almost bled to death
so he should try Ricky's on the corner.
Earl's hair was over his ears
and Mrs. Ricky, very pretty with black hair,
was sitting at the window at the manicurist's table,
shiny bottles all around her.
So he went in and she said hi
only it was Mrs. Butch not Mrs. Ricky
but he didn't know that until Butch
came from the back and said this chair.
Earl looked at his tee shirt that said
"Hail Maui, Full of Grass" and the tattoos
that rode his muscles like surfers
(one was a woman in chains)
and he said are you Ricky? And the man
said I'm Butch and he rattled the scissors
in the jar of antiseptic. So Earl
got in the chair and said don't cut much.

❧

Turned Funny

Southern women turn funny sometimes
when what the creek don't drown
the locust eat up or the sun comes up
wrong side of the house. Good women,
turned funny, like my aunt Alma who,
leaving a pot of beans to burn,
did a mean cancan out in the yard
flipping her skirt over white cotton drawers
that nearly blinded a couple of truckers.

And Southern families hold up their heads
straight as a church choir on Sunday.
"When Mama turned funny," they say proudly,
"she dived from the bannisters, smashed
the zinnias." Or "Judy sends postcards to Jesus."
And now my family, God bless them, chime in.
"Our Anne," they boast, "she writes poetry."

❧

At the Center of the Universe

Today I till my garden in the triangular patch
between the pear tree and the fence. Here
I will plant tomatoes and a row of sunflowers

that will turn on their stems toward the light.
Look at me, hands and knees black from kneeling,
breaking up clods of sweet-smelling dirt that

crumble silently, innocently as stars.
In three months hummingbirds will flame against blue
and dive to yellow-rayed flowers.

Look at me lying under the tree naming God.
See me eating a warm tomato, my mouth
opening and closing, opening and closing.

After the Bombing at Harrod's

It was like a movie, the Italian kind,
heavy with symbols like the Gourmet Food pears
ripe, yellow, we had just bought
that we carried up the stairs
to the nearest exit where two lady bobbies
screamed, "This way! This way!"

Nothing was real. I knew this and
tried to explain, holding your head
while you were sick, that the strewn bodies
were mannequins, the cries—sound effects.
Pure Fellini. Just look around.
Pigeons fanning sepia dust,
red shoes flung on glass.
Heavy symbols.

So you felt better and we walked
to Hyde Park and ate the pears that
smelled of earth, tasted, that had
deep fingernail marks, while around us
Talisman grandiflora (so the sign said)
tilted orangey-pink toward a weak sun.

Which may or may not have been real.

Flying Lessons

Let's say, for instance, and because it is true
that the woman who stepped
from the tenth floor window
was holding her skirt modestly with both hands
when she passed me looking out of the eighth.
And let's also say (I was ten) that we smiled
at each other and she mouthed "Goodbye"
while behind me my mother painted her nails
and my father studied the hotel menu.
Maybe I still trusted death. Who knows?
Or the look of wonder on the woman's face.
But I said nothing. The air still held her shape
clear as the pigeons whirring from the ledge
and I sat on the edge of the bed,
my heart hammering against its cage
while my mother came to stand by me
blowing on her nails, wondering
what all the commotion on the street was about.

When Mary Evelyn Comes to Visit

It will be October and I
will take her to the lake to see
the patch of Surprise Lilies that
bloom every fall.

The path is steep and dry,
not slippery like it is in spring
but covered with leaves and pine straw
that hide exposed rocks.
"Watch your step," I will say
as our shoes scuff up
small mounds of red and gold.

Let the sun be shining and
pebbles glistening as we
take off our shoes and wade,
feeling the water foam
around our feet and
talking of our mothers
both dead so recently.
And we will sit on the pier,
reminiscing, catching our breaths
at a sudden loud rattle, a kingfisher,
blue arrow piercing the lake.

At supper I will cut the bread
and steam will rise

from the newly baked loaf.
And we will eat it
with Mary Evelyn's peach preserves
in front of the fall's first fire.
And, as always with women,
our mothers and grandmothers
will sit beside us,
shaping our bread, our fire.

My Mother Candling Eggs

She places them carefully
on top of the small wooden box.
Each glows amber, a giant topaz,
and like a jeweler my mother
squints and cups her hands
around each globe that is pocked
as the moon, streaked with lightning.
She turns them looking for flaws,
for the egg the hen hid too long,
the nest egg. And the farm women
watch, six, eight cents as my mother
hands me the perfect ones to put
in the cotton-lined box.

Now, decades later, I cup my hands
around this memory. I am eight years old
and do not know the pain of these women
who watch so carefully and of my mother
who looks into their eyes, who will lie awake
asking the dark for answers. What I remember
is the day growing old against the store window,
shadow shapes on the wall,
and the cats moving closer to the stove
to watch with egg-shaped eyes.

The Old Woman As Rose, Mountain, Wind

1.

It is Christmas and a rose
still buds on my fence. Something
doesn't know the season, I think,
won't give in to the cold.
Arms full of Christmas greenery
I touch the flower in its pale yellow jacket
and whisper its name, a prayer.

2.

These are old mountains, rounded.
I've lived a life here, packed water
From the creek, broken garden hoes on rocks.
I've watched from my kitchen window
the seasons take us. When I was six,
Papa gave me a present, pointed
to the ridge, said, "Choose one."
And that mountain, beautiful and wild,
Became part of me. And I told Papa,
"I have swallowed the mountain,"
and he said, "What have I done."

3.

Oh, I was a mighty dancer! Light as air
And every man hearing my music. Every man
Trying to catch me until the wind at night
Whispered one name, wild and beautiful.

And we created children who danced
Like spirits, as if the earth had no corners.
So I gave them a mountain.

4.

Tonight the wind sings in the top of the firs,
and I am an old woman who forgives her body
its many pains, who decorates her mantel
with holly and ivy and listens to the wind's song
which may be a prayer for all that endures,
flower, mountain, wind, earth,
and is certainly praise for the giver.

POEMS FROM

Spraying Under the Bed for Wolves

Druid Press, 1985

The Year of Rain

1.

The gypsies, come
to harvest the potatoes,
smell the rotting vines
and drive away in
their flatbed truck
leaving Sister Ada,
old, bent,
coughing into her skirt
on the Calhoun road
where the postman finds her.

2.

When the water reaches
the gauge's red line
Bill Watkins opens the
pond's sluice gate
flooding the field
and drowning the
Baptist minister who
bobs down Kelly Creek
like the cork he
leaned from his boat to get.

3.

The morning the sun
quits trying and the stars
come out, the county commissioner

calls an emergency meeting.
Sister Ada, much improved
by the antibiotics
at Baldwin Memorial Hospital,
reads palms.
"We are all buried in starlight,"
she tells the commissioner
and he sees Sister Ada
once was very beautiful.
She traces the lines
on Bill Watkins's hand,
circling the whorls of callous.
"Everything is done by halves,"
she says and everyone remembers
being old. Outside stars fall
and puddle in the street;
the commissioner asks
the Methodist minister to pray.
Daisy Watkins hopes today
she will be able to take
her wash off the line.

Temptation

In my backyard
between the septic tank and the tool shed
is a large rabbit hole.
No one has noticed it but me.

I watch it while I
wash dishes, change diapers, cook supper.
(It is growing!)
I watch it while I
scrub the toilet, iron the shorts
and talk to a Jehovah's Witness
who wants to sell me a copy of *Awake*.
(It is moving closer!)

Today I went out at first light,
walked around its mouth.
Above me the trees whispered;
the sun stopped at the chain-link fence.
I lowered one foot into the hole
but I stumbled back, cried.
I am not bold enough
yet
for the fall.

Family Reunion

Was it you, father, who took me
to Uncle H. V.'s ? It must have been.
I remember sitting by you
in a car and there was a scar
in your cheek, tiny, deep,
as if a freckle had fallen out.
You sang "Springtime in the Rockies"
and I watched as the hole stretched and narrowed.
I remember Uncle H. V.'s.
Your mother is very old
wrapped in an afghan in August heat.
Kiss her. I do.
Grandma, watch this!
Cousin Vincent gallops by
standing on his horse's back.
Aunts and uncles all clap.
Surely it was you who took me
to the creek, who said this is where
we played when we were children.
Watch out for snakes.
But I am not sure.
What I do remember is Vincent
circling round and round the house,
Uncle Reese playing his Jew's harp,
and in the late light
the feeling that all of us
on Uncle H. V.'s porch were disappearing.

Aunt Nettie at the Well

For seventy years you have
walked this path.
Clutching your mother's skirt
you stood
on ridges of frozen mud
and watched her lower the bucket
bouncing it gently until it
turned and cut the water.
Later it was your skirt
the younger children held
while dreams clouded
your mother's waking hours.

The well, you tell me,
was your mirror.
Here, under the chinaberry
you set up your quilt frame
and met a man
come for the cool
wishing water of summer
and you married him,
driving into Iowa City
in a '36 Chevy
counting one-eyed cars
making wishes that
didn't bring him back

from the Pacific.
Now you throw chinaberries
down the well
at a thin white-haired woman
and talk of the windmill
once bigger than the moon,
of winters when the cows froze,
leaning into fences,
their eyes wide, surprised,
and summers of dry lightning
that arced like memory
from the fingertips
of your outstretched hand.

I look at the horizon
narrow as a knife
and imagine mountains
wedged into the sky,
forests that shape themselves
to swallow the wind.
You prop folded arms
on the well's curb
like a shield
grown too heavy to lift
"There's no place to hide,"
you say.

Mr. Philip Who Conjured Warts

"Let's see your hand," he said
and I held it out, ashamed
of the black seeded burrs
that covered my fingers.
He nodded his head. Sun
glinted off the yellow
John Deere letters and
oily green sweat ring
above the bib of his cap.
"A good crop," he said.
The other old men who
gathered each day
on the bench at McGough's store
agreed.

He held my hand
like a small white stone,
circling each wart
with his gnarled calloused finger.
The skin across the back
of his hand was thin,
discolored as old tissue paper.
"In two weeks the warts
will be gone." I felt nothing
but his rough damp palm
and the warmth of the sun
reflected from McGough's dirty windows.

"She don't believe you, Philip,"
Mr. Porterfield poked my leg
with his cane. Mr. Philip
folded my hand gently and
gave it back to me.
"It don't matter," he said.

Picking Tomatoes on Sand Mountain

The pickup bounces
up a corrugated road
through the patchwork, red,
gold, strips of lavender. We
touch our mouths carefully
to styrofoam cups of coffee,
sing "On the Road Again."
Then the sign "Pick Your Own"
and a million tomatoes
reflecting the sun.

We are early, the only ones.
We take our baskets, move
down the rows. Ripe tomatoes
drop with the slightest of twists.
Spaghetti sauce, I think, ketchup.

At the lip of the bluff we rest,
watch clouds bank in the west.
You bite a tomato, juice
runs down your chin. I
lie back against the warm rocks
watch hawks wheeling.

Listen, for whatever, I forgive you.

What If

Sometimes my mother would
show me the picture of her
with typhoid fever, three years old
held toward the camera in
her mother's arms. They thought
she would die; she looked like she would,
her face a Halloween mask.
But where would I be, I'd
want to know. Someone else's
little girl. Even then I knew
better than that. And what if
they'd had the price of a movie the night
I was conceived. They'd have been
at the Paramount eating popcorn
instead of in the bed on Finley Avenue
where for almost the last time
they reached for each other maybe
just because the night was warm
or maybe the neighbors were fighting.

I think about these things.
I don't know why.

To Virginia Who Walked on Her Hands

At the miracle revival
your mother found Jesus.
Standing by the tent
we watched her shake and moan
under the lighted cross
that fried night insects.

Afterward, going home,
you showed me you could
walk on your hands,
moving easily through cages
of light drawn
by shuttered windows.
One day, you said, you
would leave this town,
the crazy mother, the uncles
whose sex was the size
of dill pickles.
You laughed at my astonishment,
flipping to your feet,
crossing your heart
over newly rounded breasts.

And I believed you. I
skipped school when you married
the old man from Dallas
and I cried. But not you.

Going up the plane steps
you turned to wave, the
skirt of your white dress
fanning out like a moth.

It was the last time
I saw you. I know
your husband died
leaving you money
you spend in Monte Carlo,
that you have a man you love
and beautiful children.
I think of you often, Virginia.
If this isn't the way it turned out,
don't let me know.

Twice-risen Bread

Kneading the bread once-risen
in the chipped crockery bowl
that belonged to my grandmother
I push my fingers into tiny
prisons of air that pop and whisper
like small fires.
"Twice-risen is best,"
my long-dead Dosha says,
her hands black, puffy,
knuckles white knobs of flour.
She punches the dough;
soft blows cut quarter moons.
Her upper arms with their
beige stretch marks sway
above the board. "White folks
don't know it all." She looks
to see if my grandmother has heard.
Now I set the dough to rise again.
Across the decades Dosha hands me
a child's loaf coated with cinnamon and sugar.
"Jesus," she sings and I join in,
"Jesus, keeper of my soul."

The Ice Storm

The cherry laurel splits.
I hear a loud sigh and
look through the window as
the tree slowly divides.
Some branches hang together by habit
but ice tears them apart and the trunk
spills open, jagged, pale yellow.

Three days stranded, no lights,
no phone. Last night we
drank the last of the vodka,
today we will run out of logs.
On the sofa you huddle under
the double wedding-ring quilt.
Are you asleep? It doesn't matter.

I open the garage, walk to the tree.
Each step breaks the skin of ice.
I hear a noise at the window,
see you wrapped in the quilt.
Sleet and your image run down the pane,
freeze, mottled as a blind eye.

❧

Cleaning Out the Refrigerator

First the milk
clotted like white blood
bought three weeks ago
at Food World on special
the day I had to pay
for the lost library book.
It splashes into the sink
with loud gasping sounds.
Oh, I am getting my life together here.
Then the salad dressing
Kraft Creamy Dill
dated last December
goes into the garbage
with the half-filled jar
of green-dotted orange-cranberry relish.
What a good Christmas we had.
An almost full can of tomatoes,
apples and oranges, brown, dried,
a Ziploc bag of green liquid
(best not think of this)
stuck to a jar of honey
which needs to be kept
but goes in the garbage
like a fat tumor on a frog.
Lord, I am an avenging angel.
I put wet jars of pickles and jelly

on the counter
where I put them last year
and dampen the sponge
(the milk is still in the sink)
with the fake woodsy smell of disinfectant.
I sweep it through the refrigerator
where mildew collapses at my touch
and cut my finger on a sliver of ham
caught in the caged shelf.
No matter.
(My life will be like this shining enamel.)
Then I restack pickles, jelly,
Elsie's Tomato Relish, we will eat next summer,
close the door
and plug the cord into the socket.
God on the seventh day.

The Bridge Foursome

Shrimp salad for lunch,
wine in Waterford that
rainbows the cloth. They
talk of marriages, grandchildren,
the best place to buy shoes.

South

The sky is a blackbird's
wings enveloping me.
Soaring through black
falling upward.

Fall is early, they think.
The dogwood, already scarlet
in August, brushes the window,
red berries clicking
against the pane.

East

That moment when you
can't tell if a train
is going backward or forward.
When the train next to us moves
I always think it is ours.

They have two hundred years,
ten children, six husbands.
They have lost one child,
two breasts, two wombs.
They make lists (get suit
at cleaners, Jane's—bridge, 2/20),
vote, answer calls at the Crisis Center.

North

Suicide will get you nowhere.

Strange men walk their dreams.
They wake to steady breathing
beside them, wander dark houses.
There is something they think
they ought to remember, elusive
as a shadow a child tries to catch.
Rainbows fall to the floor.
They deal the cards. Each
opens her hands slowly.

West

*The snake plant on the cabinet
is dusty.*

Josie-in-the-morning

The water oaks talk among
themselves. They brush me
with tendrils of Spanish moss,
whisper who are you, why
are you here. I hear them
over the rasp of the roof
rusting in the nearby swamp.
It is that kind of day.

Josie-in-the-morning, your
house is gone. Here are the
double front steps curving
toward nothing; snakes sun
on the hearth. They stretch,
say yes, the place has changed.
No pretense to perfection.

Half awake, I hear kindling
spark, hear Josie measuring
corn. Slugabed, look,
God is ironing the field.
Golden shadows push through
the hay. Nervous chickens
caw Josie, Josie! She
throws them corn, brings
me a handful of sunshine
still green, she says,
but it will ripen.

Josie-in-the-morning says
old Noah went out on deck
when the ark hit Ararat and
right on top of that rainbow
guess what he saw?
A dove?
Judy Garland!
Aunt Josie, that's not funny.
And we laugh until the porch shakes
and chickens run from under the floor.
We remember, say the hawks,
still wheeling.

Now I sit on Josie's steps,
listen. The sun, red, pulpy,
falls through the trees.
Yes, says the swamp
leaning forward in darkness.

POEMS FROM

Wild Goose Chase

Druid Press, 1982

Big Swamp

Black and fat
Big Swamp coils
like a moccasin
around our land.
At night I hear it breathe.

> *The trees are witches, child.*
> *Look how their gray hair*
> *stirs in the wind.*
> *Hear them whisper*
> *their secrets.*

I walk the fence
that protects our cows.
My boots mire
in mud thick as tar.
I lift them heavily
scrape black clots
on the rail.

> *Listen, child, dark nights*
> *the panther screams*
> *like a woman.*
> *Your granddaddy*
> *went to hunt her*
> *and I waited*
> *until day spread*
> *like a stain.*

Every day I stare
down the path
at mist rising cool, hypnotic.
The swamp stops breathing, waits,
I pause, turn away.
Behind me I sense shadows fattening.

Going Home

South of Montgomery along the interstate
red-tailed hawks perch on bare trees
and watch the traffic pushing through
the heaviness of late fall rain.
Tonight I will lie in my mother's
spare bedroom and listen to pecans
pelting the roof with the circular
sound of giant periods.

My mother says she was whistling
when they came to tell her
my grandmother was dead. I don't know
why this bothers her or why
she takes the memory out so often
to study it like a map, carefully, intently.
I would welcome a whistle, wrap
it around me like a silver cord,
weightless, cool. But not my mother.

Which is fine. For her each morning
the sky is real and the sun is real.
She thinks she is real so she
cleans her house and never wears
patent leather shoes after five.
And this is fine. Once in Miami she

made bathtub gin, danced, barricaded
her house against the hurricane of '28.
Afterwards, the arms and legs reaching
through sand. Were they too real? Did
they follow her back to Alabama demanding
burial each day in a world of order?

Now, past the Davenport-Letohatchie exit
I know she is waiting. And the lights
will be on and supper ready.
A middle-aged child, I will become
for a while what she thinks I am,
and tomorrow, wading through mounds
of damp leaves, bundled against the wind,
we will fill croaker sacks with pecans
and then take them in and shell them
as we do every November for the winter
my mother says will come.

Aunt Edith

In heat of summer
only you can breathe here
propped in your chair,
legs and feet floating.
Always your Bible
(how can you see)
while you hook our arms
with veined fingers
whispering, "are you saved?"

Once starch bright
you sat on a pony laughed
into a picture wedded
a man who called you "Trigger."
One April you drove a Model A
two hundred miles down dirt roads
to see the ocean.

When did earth become heavy?
Surely God in your kitchen
retreating to heaven
up years of empty soup cans
explained the cocoon comes first.
Grappling for him, terrified,
did you hear?

Now in your room
waiting heaven
you peel the days away
calling to us as we sneak by,
"are you saved, are you saved?"

August

Summer has been here a
long time. Under the East Pass bridge
the dune curves like
a question mark and forms
a shallow bay. In the
marsh grass gulls stand in
clusters rocking gently to the
wake of fishing boats. Tonight
I will scoop out a bowl
in the sand, lie there
and watch the Perseids burn
holes with green torches.
The sky is falling.
The sky is falling.
No use telling the king.
A line of brown pelicans
skims across the water
and each night now the earth
tilts deeper into dark lavender space.

I Can Almost Believe

All afternoon, driving through
thick mountain clouds, carefully
following the road that ends in
mist, I can almost believe
we have found the flaw in time.
Quietness envelops us, cliffs
cease to exist, and trees distorted
by fog loom and disappear.

I know that soon the
clouds will begin to thin
and the sun will appear
a pale yellow disc. I
know that the road will
turn downward and the
earth resume its familiar
face. And we who have
lived together so long will
stop for the night and take
our bags into a motel room
like all others and sit
across a table at supper,
our faces familiar masks.

But I also know that tonight
lying in a strange bed
staring into the spaces between
sleep, I will see your hands
on the wheel, beautiful,
veins crisscrossing like the lines
on the map that lies between us.

Emily Your Name

Emily your name will
once again be yours. Today
you cry and say great-grandmother

has stolen it. But it is
only borrowed. This I
promise you. It will

not be long that she dresses it in old lady
clothes of gray and mauve,

crochets with it, makes
it sleep with Kleenex,
teeth, glasses. For a name

does not remain faithful
to the redness of old skin,
smell of medicine, chill, pain.

It is easily seduced
by the softness of a young
lover's tongue. One day

soon it will return
naked, malleable, make
its home so deep inside your

head that people looking into
your eyes will mistake it
for you and say, "Emily."

Settling Aunt Annie's Estate

All day we have unraveled
her life,
winding it around us.
Now pictures, cloths, quilts
bind us to her.
Our faces are accusing mirrors
we turn to the wall.

The April sun is warm.
By the front walk
the crabapple tree
that Aunt Annie loved
and Uncle Harry cursed each fall
while raking in tiny apples
is blooming.
We walk under its canopy,
the scent of roses
stitching us
like needles.

I place a box of dishes
in my car
and remember once
I saw my aunt
hit my uncle with a broom
and then go inside
and bake a pie.

She brought him a piece
handing him the plate gently
and for an instant both
held the plate trembling
between them.
And I remember their son
and how he went
to the basement one day,
spread newspapers on the floor
and shot himself, simply, neatly.

Our work finished
we come together
surprising ourselves
with embraces
that hurt our breasts.
Innocent dreamers
caught in the thread
of the wrong dream,
we stand quietly while
the late afternoon sun
crisscrosses our shadows
thin and fragile
as new grass.

Canoeing to Goat Island

Moon still visible in the west,
we drag our canoe across the beach
and push off through fog
that outlines the banks.
Tongues of pine follow us
into the current and past
occasional houses where people dream
the silver thrust of our oars.

Your thin shoulders
bend to the rowing. In
growing light objects drift past,
log with sleeping turtles,
cemetery with its last gray stone
touching the water's edge. You
point to a rock,
a raccoon breakfasting on mussels,
neat pile of shells surrounding him.

A boat whines past and fades;
concentric waves catch us.
We rise and fall
white lace folding around us
and at each rising
and falling

a moment
turning toward nothing
the heart swelled,
still,
rehearsing.

Now your oar pushes us forward
past outcropping stone.
A startled kingfisher complains.
I smile at his squawks
then dip my oar into the water
and row toward Goat Island
as a chord of sun crests the horizon.

My Mother's Letters

From the cedar chest
the fox fur's amber eyes
glare at me. I give
them back the charge
they have guarded
for my lifetime, pushing
the package under mothballs
specific as bones.
But penciled words
awake now
stir
decades from their dreams

> . . . please don't leave me,
> don't take Anne . . .

Biplanes crossed
the two-cent stamps
that summer of the Great Depression.
In a few years the world
would fight a war
and the moon would rise and
the sun set across the pastures.
I would look across them and
try to imagine war.

> . . . just let Anne
> scratch on some paper
> and send it to me so
> I will know she is well . . .

"Tell me about him."
"There's nothing to tell,"
and the shadow man
stirring—nothing, nothing.

"Is this his picture?"
A tall man, face shaded,
wind blowing his tie.
"I told you there's nothing to tell."

>   . . . the bank of Bay Biscayne
>   closed last week. I have
>   only ten dollars to send . . .

Hate, someone else's
burst and killed six million Jews.
My mother worked at the post office
(she sorted mail for forty years)
until the fingers of her right hand
crossed like scissors.
In death they clutched at her dress.

Now in the late
last spring of day
the smell of mothballs
clings to my hands,
in the distance I hear trains switching.
Soon it will be night
and the family I love
will sit around the table
faces half shadowed
by the overhead light,
words forming pictures
diffused as flowers under glass.
How simple.
We are sentenced
to bury each other
again and again.

Quilting

We sit at the frame
three women backstitching,
eight stitches to an inch
the way our grandmother
taught us. Alternating
triangles of "Heaven and Earth"
reflect and shadow afternoon sun
and the radio plays softly as we
talk about the yellow material
from Alice's skirt and how it looks
next to the dark blue with roses.

Soon we will straighten fingers
just beginning to gnarl,
stretch our backs and go home
to fix supper for the husbands
we married thirty years ago.

But not for a while.

The sun gathers golden
in my sister's parlor and
dust motes sparkle in the
slanting light. Dishwashers,
grown children, and darkness
seem far away. We
place the triangles together
as we have done so often
and stitch, thimbles blinking
lights across the pattern.